Ethereal Land

A story of loss, a story of gain

Linda Ruth Brooks

Dedicated to my father, Max Brooks,
who lived real, and to the grandson
who made his last years shine.

Introduction

If you have ever had to tell your child that they have "lost" a loved one, struggled to come to terms with your own grief, as well as explain the awful phenomenon of death, then you have stood in my shoes. And your heart has burst, with a yearning to hold on and convey the concept of a loving God, in the midst of a Godless nightmare.

The desire of my own heart has prompted me to write a story in children's terms about the reality of an ever-loving God, whose heart longs to reunite all of his children, with each other and himself.

I wrote this story for my son, but also for all the boys and girls who have ever lost anyone or anything. I have also written for all the parents, who have sat across the breakfast table with hearts heavy with the longing to help their children know God and love Him.

This is for all the parents who have said, 'Eat everything on your plate,' when the real words hovering in the air were, 'For you, my child, and your future—I ache'. For all the parents who have said, 'Be careful!' but really wanted to say, 'Today, and every day, go with God'.

How little of what we really want to say is communicated to our children. We are so concerned with what they are doing; we lose sight of who they are becoming.

So if this book says any of the things that you long to say to your child then I will say, 'Today, and every day, go with God'.

Linda Ruth Brooks

There once was a land called Ethereal Land.

It was a very strange place; very hard to describe to people. One really couldn't understand it unless they had lived there for some time. Even then, some people who had lived there for a lifetime never really knew what it was all about.

It was made of cloud and mist. Although it looked firm and solid, there was something different about the whole place. Of course, the bricks looked like bricks and the houses really did look like houses. However, people couldn't understand the difference and couldn't explain it.

They had the feeling that when things looked most real, they might somehow fade away. Things in Ethereal Land felt as though they really existed, but something always made people wonder.

The truth about Ethereal Land was that it wasn't quite real. Because the people had never known anything else, they couldn't believe there was anything more real than their world. Everyone went about their daily routine, and didn't think much about it. Life was busy. The days were full. What difference did it make anyway?

Most people in Ethereal Land had vague thoughts about its realness.

But anyone looking who knew what *was* real, could see that none of the things keeping people busy were real at all. The people just looked like mime artists on an empty stage, acting out non~existent lives.

If you asked anyone what they were doing, they would look at you oddly and not even bother to answer. They couldn't believe anything could be more real. There couldn't be anything more at all. Such thoughts were nonsense.

Not all the people in Ethereal Land were like this. There were those who dared to say, 'Nothing is real here, the Real world is yet to come.' They were called the Credente. They talked of a better land; far away. A land where beauty shined in every corner, where happiness was everywhere and pain was a shadowy memory.

In Ethereal Land, they saw glimpses of that other world, in the song of the birds, in the glassy ripples of the water and the shifting blues of the sky; but most of all in the songs of love in their hearts. The Credente said all these things pointed to the Real One, but they were widely ignored and usually mocked.

In Ethereal Land lived an old man named Chard.

He lived with his five year old grandson Seth. They were as close as two people can be who only have each other.

Chard was a Credente. He explained to Seth that the things around them weren't truly real. He spoke of how they must live in Ethereal Land until the Real One, who had made all things, would take his people to the Real World to live with him.

This greatly puzzled Seth. Why nothing could be more real than his teddy bear Danthon. He just couldn't understand how a world yet to come, could be more real than his furry friend. He was busy being a boy, playing on the swing Grandpapa made and building miniature towns for his toys.

One day Seth pulled at his grandfather's sleeve, 'Grandpapa, what *is* Real?'

'Real is for always. If anything isn't for always, why then it's just not Real.' Chard placed a strong work-worn hand over Seth's heart to place something important there. Seth looked up. Would he ever understand? Resting his small hand over Chard's large one, he smiled. That was real enough for now.

ne day Chard had to leave the village and find work

He had to go to another part of Ethereal Land. He tried to explain to Seth why they must go there, but Seth thought it all sounded like adult nonsense. *He would not go!*

There were no words to convince Seth. The more Chard pleaded, the more stubborn and determined Seth became. Chard could not, would not force, but he was wise and knew they must go. Picking up Seth's teddy bear Danthon, he quietly walked away down the road.

Seth's face changed and disbelief filled his eyes.

'Grandpapa!' he called. Suddenly, the playhouse and the shaded swing behind the cottage seemed less real, less beckoning. His whole heart longed for his Grandpapa. Anxious little legs carried him along the rocky path, until with grazed knees he caught up with his beloved Grandpapa.

'My love for you is real, you know, Grandpapa—more real than anything,' Seth said, 'And, Grandpapa, *Danthon is real, and he loves me too!'*

As Seth grew up Chard told him more about the Real One.

The one who would someday bring the Real world.

He explained how the Real One would fill all the empty places in people's hearts and take away all their tears and sadness.

Seth didn't think he had any "empty places" Grandpapa always dried his tears.

There were times Seth questioned these things, but he couldn't tell his grandpapa he didn't understand. Why, there were so many questions, and too few answers. He didn't really disbelieve, he just didn't feel a need inside of him. He played with his friends, fished in the rippling creek behind the cottage he shared with Grandpapa.

Seth knew he once had a mother and father, but he didn't remember them. Life with Chard was all he had ever known. As Chard tucked him into bed at night with Danthon, his teddy bear, he couldn't imagine how there could be anything more.

Seth watched his Grandpapa with the other men of the Credente. Sometimes they came to visit the cottage. They were his friends too. What else could a boy want?

Now, a very strange thing happened in Ethereal Land.

People disappeared. It was well known everyone had to leave one day, but there was confusion about where they went. Sometimes people disappeared suddenly, but other times they simply faded, becoming more and more see-through.

Some said the Real One took them, others said an evil prince came, but most times the Real One was blamed, even by people who didn't believe. The Credente sometimes wondered when they sat with broken hearts, what it was all about?

These things didn't bother Seth too much for he had now become a man and was very busy with the business and plans of Ethereal Land. He didn't often think about the Real One who loved you like a father and was someone you could love too. It just seemed like a childhood story he'd outgrown long ago. He forgot all about the Credente. Now Seth was respected by people around him.

Seth even began to think he had been responsible for creating the things he owned. The things he did and the life he had, seemed like the only real things.

But then Seth began to notice subtle changes in Chard.

He seemed a little more faded. He pushed these things to the back of his mind and returned to his "busyness".

The day came when he could hide from the truth no longer. When he visited Chard in the chill of the early autumn days, he found him sitting under the oak tree by the quiet riverbank behind his cottage. Seth sensed something in the air; a heaviness. Then he knew; his beloved grandpapa was definitely disappearing. He saw in Chard's eyes a world of love, promise, joy and sadness.

All the words Seth ever wanted to say crowded tightly together, staying in one big lump in his throat. When he tried to speak, only a growly sound came out, but he didn't need to say anything.

Grandpapa's eyes held a lifetime of understanding and love.

Seth sobbed, 'What are the answers, Grandpapa?'

Instinctively Chard knew the questions. He struggled to explain things he only dimly understood, but trusted, believed—the important things in an unreal world.

emember when we had to leave our village when you were only five?' Chard began. 'Well, it's a little bit like that now. The Real One doesn't take anyone away, but when we lose someone, he yearns with all his great heart that we will long after the one we have lost, with a love stronger than anything else and find what is Real. He calls us to travel along a path where all the things of Ethereal Land will fade from our minds. He longs for us to call him Father and to call home ~ where he is.'

Chard paused. He reached out to Seth. Then, with his work roughened hand, Chard wiped away the very real tears flowing down Seth's sad face.

'The love that burns brightly in here,' he said, placing his hand over his own heart, 'is a mirror of all the love He is and ever will be. When all our journeys end, when every story has been told, He will take us home. To fill all the empty places in our hearts, taking away our tears and giving our loved ones back into our longing arms.'

'You once believed your teddy bear's love was real, but it was just a shadow of my love for you. Now believe that the Real One loves you "this many".'

Chard held up all ten gnarled fingers, in the familiar gesture of Seth's childhood, and said, *'All this many.'*

efore he disappeared, Chard gave Seth one last loving look. He gently placed a tattered envelope in Seth's trembling hands. It was his last gift to his grandson. 'I cannot leave you any of the things of Ethereal Land; but I can leave you the most real thing of all—love,' Chard murmured. 'Whenever you feel love, you will remember me and I will never be far away. That is what is *Real*.'

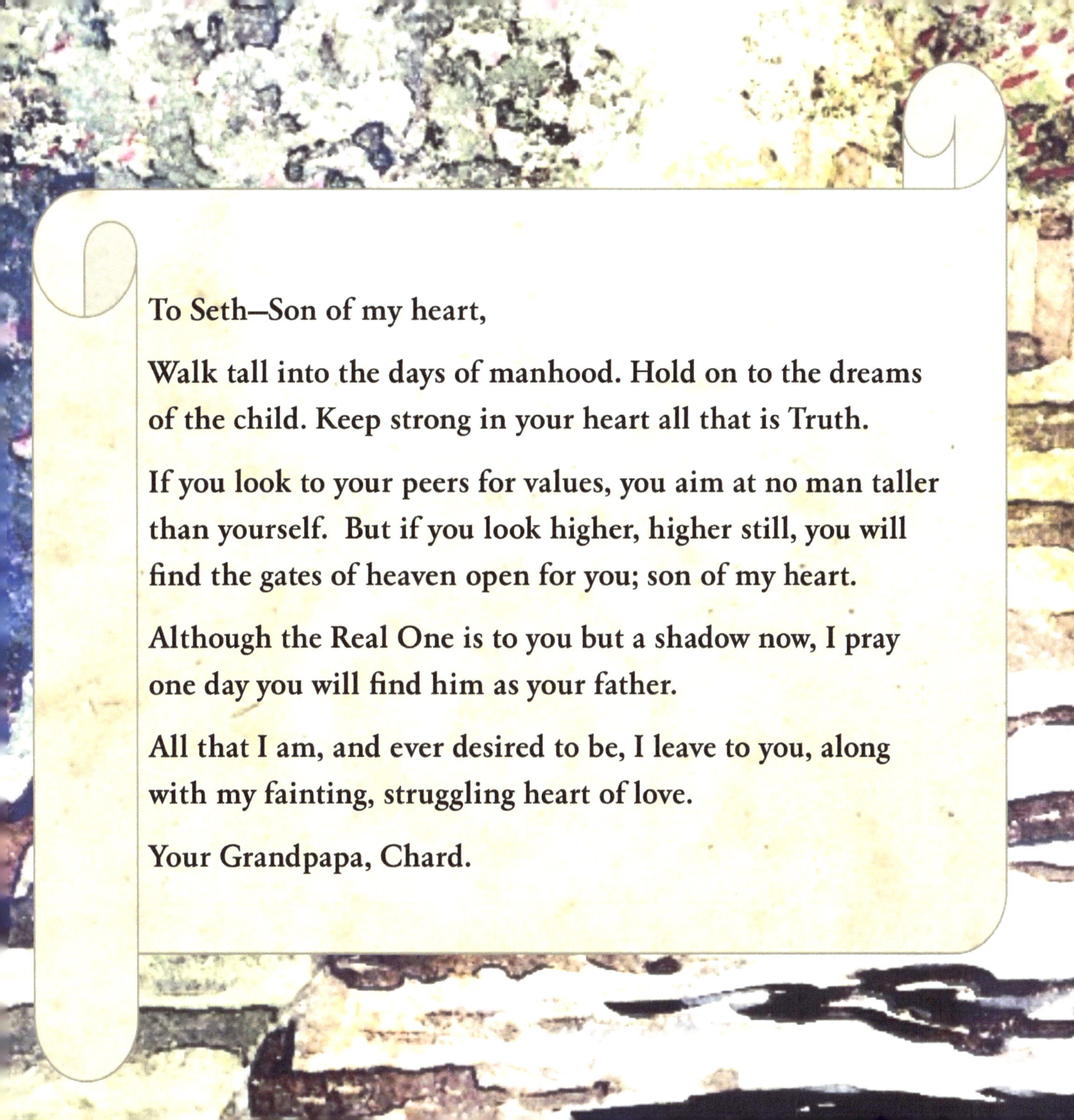

To Seth—Son of my heart,

Walk tall into the days of manhood. Hold on to the dreams of the child. Keep strong in your heart all that is Truth.

If you look to your peers for values, you aim at no man taller than yourself. But if you look higher, higher still, you will find the gates of heaven open for you; son of my heart.

Although the Real One is to you but a shadow now, I pray one day you will find him as your father.

All that I am, and ever desired to be, I leave to you, along with my fainting, struggling heart of love.

Your Grandpapa, Chard.

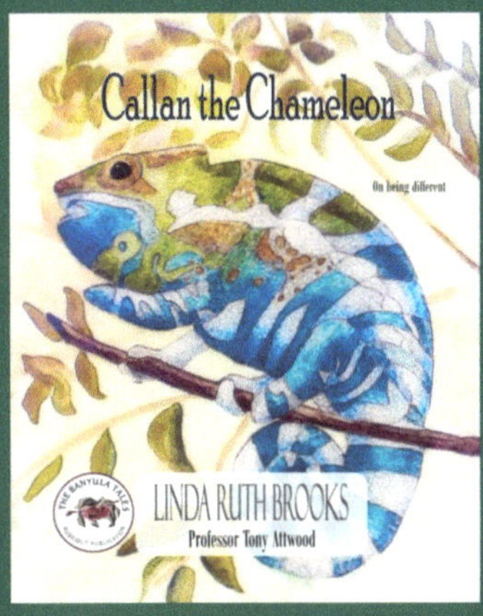

Callan the Chameleon
On being different
LINDA RUTH BROOKS
Professor Tony Attwood

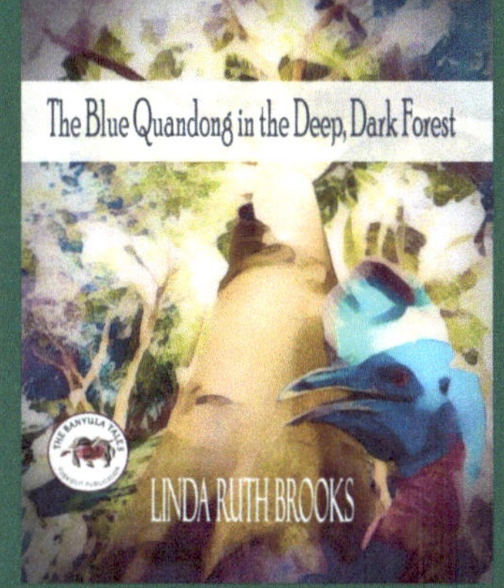

The Blue Quandong in the Deep, Dark Forest
LINDA RUTH BROOKS

Banyula's Angry Birds Get Mean
LINDA RUTH BROOKS

Blue Roo Gives a Stranger a Name
Making friends
LINDA RUTH BROOKS

The Clouds Fall on Banyula
LINDA RUTH BROOKS

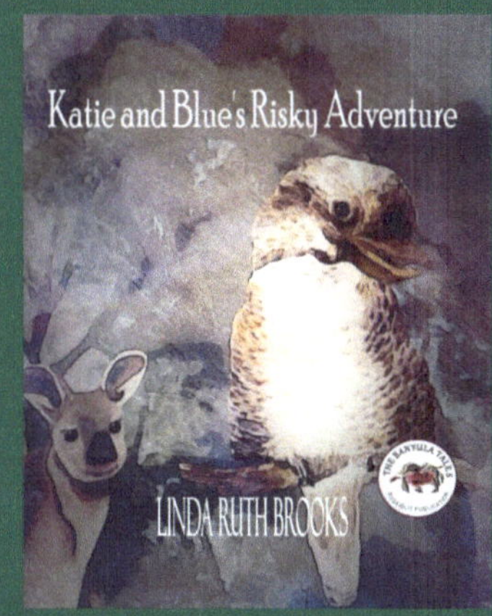

Katie and Blue's Risky Adventure
LINDA RUTH BROOKS

Christmas Chaos Comes to Banyula
Community
LINDA RUTH BROOKS

The frog that hiccupped
LINDA RUTH BROOKS

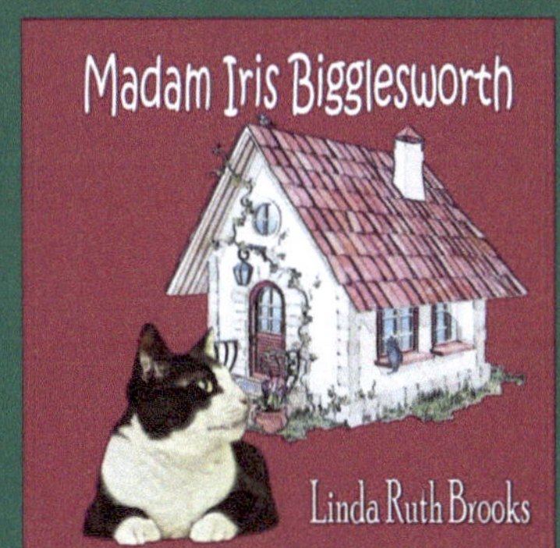

Madam Iris Bigglesworth
Linda Ruth Brooks

A tabby never forgets
LINDA RUTH BROOKS

Four Sneaky Kittens
Violet Elizabeth Crabtree

Beth's Christmas Wish
LINDA RUTH BROOKS

Cover Design by Linda Brooks
Original Artwork © Linda Brooks

ISBN-9798825175614
Fiction/juvenile/mind, body, spirit
Author website: **http://www.lindaruthbrooks.com/**

Ethereal Land is a work of fiction. Any similarity between the characters in this book and real people, living or dead, is coincidental.

This book, and others by Linda, can be purchased at
online bookstores, retail outlets.

www.ingramcontent.com/pod-product-compliance
Lightning Source LLC
Chambersburg PA
CBHW042141030726
47599CB00002B/570